DATE DUE

APR. 1 8 1983	AY 1 5		
JAN. 2 1 1984			
FEB 1 5 1984			
AG 1 6 '86			
FE 1 5 '92			
FE 24 '92			
SEP 23 94			
DEC 28			
MO 21 01			
JA 31 02			
AP 07 04			
OC 19 09			

FAMOUS NAMES IN WORLD EXPLORATION

JAMES HEWITT

Wayland

ISBN 0 85340 549 2
© Copyright 1979 Wayland Publishers Ltd
First published in 1979 by
Wayland Publishers Limited
49 Lansdowne Place, Hove
East Sussex, BN3 1HF, England.
Printed by Cahills, Dublin—Second impression 1981

CONTENTS

MARCO POLO
the first European in the East

In 1260, Nicolo and Maffeo Polo, merchants of Venice
seeking trade, journeyed thousands of kilometres to Peking.
This was the capital of the Mongol empire which stretched
from the Pacific to the Mediterranean. Kublai Khan, the ruler,
gave them a letter to the Pope asking that a hundred men of
religion, the arts, and science should be sent to China.

The brothers were away nine years, but they set out to the
East again in 1272. The Pope sent only two friars, who soon
took fright and turned back. Nicolo's seventeen-year-old son
Marco did not turn back. He was gripped by the many
wonders he saw and took note of them all on a journey that
lasted three-and-a-half years and took him through Palestine,
Armenia, Persia, to Baghdad and the Persian Gulf, across the
wide Gobi Desert, to China, Peking and the magnificent court
of Kublai Khan.

Marco worked seventeen years for the Khan, as governor of
the city of Yangchow, and on special missions to the Chinese
provinces, Burma, and Ceylon. He never lost his sense of
wonder.

When the Polos returned to Venice, this time mainly by sea,
they were not recognized at first. It is said they slit the seams
of their Tartar robes and out showered precious stones.

Marco's stories of his travels were published—but few
believed them. Man-eating serpents? (alligators). Stones that
burned? (coal). It was a hundred years before map-makers
realized that Marco had told the truth and began filling in
some of the blank spaces on the map of Asia. *The Travels of
Marco Polo* inspired other explorers for several centuries,
including Christopher Columbus. He took a well-thumbed
copy with him on his voyage to the New World. Some of the
places Marco Polo had been were not seen by another
European for 500 years.

4

CHRISTOPHER COLUMBUS
the discoverer of America

Christopher Columbus, an Italian, spent ten years looking for support for his exciting idea. He wanted to reach the rich East by sailing west across the Atlantic from Europe. Finally, he persuaded Ferdinand and Isabella, the rulers of Spain, to pay for an expedition.

In September 1492, Columbus commanded three small ships, with 120 men, that sailed west from the Canary Islands. The continent of America did not appear on the maps.

When thirty-three days passed without sight of land, Columbus's crews were close to mutiny. But on 12th October, 1492 Columbus set foot on Watling Island, in the Bahamas, and went on to Cuba. He thought he had reached Asia. Even today the islands Columbus found are called the West Indies, and the natives of America are called Indians.

For his second voyage in September 1493, Columbus had seventeen ships and about 1,500 men. He discovered Dominica, Guadeloupe, Martinique, Puerto Rico, and Jamaica. But when this visit to the West Indies failed to produce the gold, silver, and precious stones Columbus had talked about, the interest of the King and Queen weakened.

For a third expedition, Columbus was allowed only six ships. He discovered Trinidad in 1498 and reached the American mainland, sailing along the coast of Venezuela. He was a dreamer rather than a practical man and made a poor governor of the lands he discovered. He returned to Spain in some disgrace in November 1500.

He had to pay himself for his fourth and final voyage. This time he reached the coast of Honduras and followed the coastline south as far as the Isthmus of Panama. His fame had faded and he was in poor health. He retired in Spain and died there in 1506, wealthy but not fantastically rich, and without the fame as the discoverer of America the history books would later give him.

In the picture below, Columbus presents an account of his first voyage to the King and Queen of Spain.

VASCO DA GAMA
a trade route by sea to the East

As a boy Vasco da Gama dreamed of becoming a great sea captain. He grew up at a time when Portuguese navigators were adding new places to the map of Africa and Portuguese settlements were being set up along the coast. He studied navigation and went on various voyages to learn seamanship.

In February 1488, Bartolomeo Dias showed that there was a gateway to the East via the southernmost tip of the continent of Africa. In 1497, King Emanuel of Portugal asked Vasco da Gama to make the Lisbon-India voyage. With four ships and 118 men, he sailed from Lisbon on 8th July and was without sight of land for ninety days before reaching South Africa and rounding the Cape of Good Hope on 22nd November. It took two attempts to get through the currents between Mozambique and Madagascar. But with the monsoon favouring them, they crossed the Indian Ocean in twenty-three days, to reach Calicut, on the south-west coast of India, on 23rd May, 1498. The Portuguese explorers had some trouble with the ruler of Calicut, and when they eventually left they had to fight their way out of the harbour.

Da Gama was able to load his ships with spices. The passage back to Portugal was a battle against tropical heat, opposing winds, sickness, and fatigue. Da Gama reached Lisbon in September 1499, and was welcomed by cheering crowds. Less than sixty of the fleet's original 118 men had survived. They had sailed 24,000 nautical miles in 630 days.

Da Gama's pioneer voyage to India had important results. Several more journeys were to follow. He had opened a new route for European merchant ships to trade with the East. Prosperous trading centres like Alexandria, Venice and Genoa, that had served the old routes to the East, began to decline. Land travel to the East was also on the decline; it began to be replaced by sea travel.

9

FRANCISCO PIZARRO
and the conquest of the Incas

Hernando Cortes (see page 14) destroyed the Aztec civilization of Mexico. A few years later Francisco Pizarro destroyed another fantastically rich American civilization—that of the Incas of Peru. He twice sailed from Panama to Peru to make sure the stories of gold and silver were true. Then he persuaded King Charles V of Spain to supply soldiers and ships for the conquest of Peru. Like Cortes, Pizarro had a small force: 3 ships, 180 men, and 27 horses.

The Inca empire stretched for 3,000 km along the high plateau of the Andes. Pizarro's small army climbed from equatorial heat into cold mountain snows. On 15th November, 1532 they reached the city of Cuxamalca. The Peruvian army of 40,000 men was encamped outside the city. Atahuallpa, the Inca or Emperor, was with his army. Pizarro sent peaceful greetings from the mighty Spanish emperor far across the world. The Inca was carried ceremoniously on a litter to the central plaza of the city. Pizarro gave a signal, and twenty-seven horsemen led an attack on the Peruvians, who had never seen horses. The firing of the Spanish cannon caused even greater panic. 10,000 Peruvians were slaughtered, and their Emperor captured. Pizarro offered to spare Atahuallpa's life for gold heaped as high as the Emperor could reach. Atahuallpa was tall, but was made to stand on tiptoe. A room seven metres long and five metres wide was heaped with gold to a height of nearly three metres. Despite his promise, Pizarro then had the Emperor strangled. He conquered Cuzco, the Peruvian capital, with little difficulty. In December 1533 he crowned a new Lord Inca who would co-operate with the Spanish conquistadors.

Pizarro founded Lima as his capital city and ruled like a king. He had a rival Spaniard put to death. Friends of the rival attacked and killed Pizarro at Lima on 26th June, 1541.

FERDINAND MAGELLAN
first around the world

Ferdinand Magellan, a Portuguese navigator, was asked by King Charles V of Spain to search for a south-west passage from the Atlantic to the Pacific and to bring back spices from the Moluccas.

He sailed with five ships and about 270 men from San Lucar on 20th September, 1519. He followed the east coast of South America, determined if necessary to go into the Antarctic Circle. The crews suffered great hardships from the cold. On 1st April, 1520 some of the sailors mutinied and seized three of the five ships, but the mutiny was put down. Then one ship hit a shoal and sank. On 22nd May, Magellan found that dishonest traders had only supplied half the food paid for; there was only enough to last six months. He did not tell his crews.

They spent two winter months anchored in the mouth of the Santa Cruz River, at 50° South. At the first signs of spring, they sailed south again, and in only three days, on 21st October, 1520 they discovered the strait they had been seeking. It is still called Magellan Strait. It twists and turns for 515 km and the usual winds are western. It took Magellan thirty-eight days to get through to the Pacific Ocean. One ship deserted and turned back.

In crossing the Pacific, the three remaining small ships sailed for ninety-eight days without finding land. The starving crews ate rats, leather, and sawdust. Nineteen sailors died; more were ill. In January 1521 they reached the Philippines. Magellan did not return to Spain to the welcome he deserved. He was caught up in a fight between natives and was killed.

At the Moluccas, the crew of one ship deserted and so did half of another. Sebastian del Cano brought one ship, the *Victoria*, back to Spain, with only eighteen men. They had been away three years and had sailed right round the world.

13

HERNANDO CORTES
conqueror of the Aztecs

At the age of nineteen, Hernando Cortes went from Spain to the West Indies, which were discovered by Christopher Columbus (see page 6) only twelve years before. "I come to get gold, not to till the soil like a peasant," he said. His wish came true when in 1519 he commanded a small force of Spaniards who landed in Mexico and destroyed—by a combination of cruelty, trickery, and bravery—the rich civilization of the Aztecs. Cortes was certainly brave—he burned the ships that took the expedition to Mexico so that none of his men could turn back.

Cortes had about 500 men, 15 horses, 13 muskets, and 7 small cannon with which to overcome many thousands of Aztecs. But he was greatly helped by two things. The Aztecs were terrified of the guns and the horses, neither of which they had seen before. Even more helpful was the legend of a departed Aztec god, Quetzalcoatl, who had disappeared across the Atlantic but was due to return the very year Cortes landed. The Aztec King, Montezuma, thought Cortes must be Quetzalcoatl, and allowed the Spaniards to enter Mexico city. It was built in a lake and surrounded by causeways. When one of the Spaniards was murdered, Cortes seized Montezuma and put him in chains. He occupied Mexico city for six months and was severe with the Aztecs, who rose against him. Montezuma was killed. Cortes and his men had to fight their way out of the city by night along the causeways. Cortes lost many men, but took bloody revenge when, with the help of enemies of the Aztecs, he attacked Mexico city in May 1521. After fierce fighting, the Aztecs surrendered on 13th August.

Cortes governed the country for seven years. He became so powerful that the Spanish government became fearful and eventually he was sent back to Spain, and died poor and neglected near Seville.

15

JACQUES CARTIER
the discoverer of Canada

In 1534, King Francis I of France sent Cartier across the Atlantic, with two ships, to search for the North-West Passage—a way through North America from the Atlantic to the Pacific. It would open a new sea route to Asia. He sailed south along the coasts of Labrador and western Newfoundland. He entered the wide mouth of the St Lawrence without realizing there was a river. He landed at Cape Gaspé, planted a cross, and took possession of the land in the name of the King of France. The Indians he met were friendly and he took two of them back to France for the interest of the King.

Cartier sailed to Canada again in the following year. This time he discovered the St Lawrence River and sailed up it as far as the Indian village of Stadacona, now Quebec. He used two small boats to go up-river to a village by a hill which he named Mont Real—the site of the present city of Montreal. He returned to France in the summer of 1536. This time he took two Indian chiefs.

Cartier commanded a fleet of five ships which sailed from France to Canada in the spring of 1541. The expedition was a disaster. Many of Cartier's men were killed by Indians. He took back to France what he thought were precious stones, which turned out to be only iron pyrites and mica.

But as a result of Cartier's three voyages to Canada, map-makers had reliable knowledge of parts of Canada, and explorers, traders and missionaries would eventually follow Cartier's lead. An attempt at colonization failed by 1543; but sixty-five years later Samuel de Champlain (see page 18) founded Quebec and began to build New France in the territory along the St Lawrence which Cartier had discovered. Jacques Cartier died in St Malo, where he had been born, in 1557.

17

SAMUEL DE CHAMPLAIN
the father of New France

Samuel de Champlain was the leading figure in North
American exploration during the first half of the seventeenth
century. Jacques Cartier (see page 16) had opened the way
for the French in Canada. Champlain has been called the
father of New France. New France was the name given to the
province of Quebec in the early days of its settlement.

He made his first voyage to the St Lawrence River in 1603
and in the next two years explored the coasts of Nova Scotia
and southwards as far as Cape Cod. He surveyed, made maps
and chose places for French families to set up homes. The first
group of families journeyed with Champlain from France to
Canada in 1608. That year he founded Quebec. As the settlers
were building homes, Champlain joined an Indian war party
and shared their battles and hardships. His musket terrified
the enemy Indians. On this journey he went south from the St
Lawrence along the Richelieu River to the lake which bears his
name.

Champlain returned several times to France to raise money
for New France from wealthy nobles and to bring over more
families. He set up a trading post at Montreal in 1611, and
was made Lieutenant Governor of New France the next year.
He governed the colony well and still found time for more
journeys into the unknown West. He canoed far up the Ottawa
River and on another journey reached Lake Huron and
explored much of the country near Lake Ontario. Missionary
priests went with Champlain on some of his later explorations.

In 1629 he was captured by the British and taken to
England. He spent his time as a prisoner writing about his
explorations. On release, he returned to Quebec, where he
died in 1635.

The French influence in Quebec and Montreal is strong
even today.

19

JAMES COOK
discoverer of Australia

James Cook, the son of a Yorkshire farm worker, had little education, but became one of the most skilful navigators in history. He was a natural leader. There was not the great loss of life among his sailors that was usual on long voyages in the eighteenth century, because he made sure their living quarters were kept clean and well-ventilated and that they always had fresh meat, fruit, and vegetables.

Because he had made an excellent survey of Canada, Cook was appointed commander of what was said to be a scientific expedition to Tahiti to study the transit of the planet Venus. Secretly, it was to search for a *Terra Australis* or Southern Land long believed to exist in the southern hemisphere. He was to claim it for Britain, along with any undiscovered islands found on the way.

Cook sailed from Plymouth in the *Endeavour* in July 1768. Venus passed across the sun in April 1769. Cook then went on his secret mission. He reached New Zealand in October and charted 4,000 km of the eastern coastline and established that New Zealand was two islands.

He sailed west and reached the eastern coast of Australia, which he named New South Wales. In April 1770, he landed at Botany Bay. He named Port Jackson, the site of the present city of Sydney. The *Endeavour* ran aground on the Great Barrier Reef, but Cook skilfully saved the ship. He recognized that Australia was a very suitable land for people from Britain to go and live. The first colonists—convicted criminals—landed at Botany Bay in January 1788.

In 1779, Captain Cook was killed by natives in Hawaii, which he had discovered—a sad end for a man who had always been friendly with the natives of the lands and islands he had discovered.

ALEXANDER MACKENZIE
and the exploration of Canada

Alexander Mackenzie, a Scots-Canadian, was the first white man to travel overland, canoeing and portaging, from the settlements on the St Lawrence River in eastern Canada to the Pacific Ocean in the west. He made the journey of exploration on behalf of his employers, the North-West Company of Canada, which was formed by fur-traders in 1783.

He started by canoe from Peace River on 12th October, 1792. He was accompanied by a small party of men. They canoed up the river until forced to make a nineteen-kilometre portage. They reached a point where the Peace River forked into the Finlay River and the Parsnip River and navigated the latter, following it to a lake.

The picture below is a painting by John David Kelley of Sir Alexander Mackenzie's first glimpse of the Pacific Ocean.

Some of the Indians Mackenzie met were friendly, but others were hostile. His men sometimes became bad-tempered over the hardships of the journey and talked of turning back. They crossed the great Rocky Mountains to the Fraser River. They began to go down the river, but turned back because some Indians warned of great difficulties ahead.

Mackenzie now explored south until he found the Bellacoola River. This time he was more successful, for it took him to his goal—the Pacific Ocean. On a rock at Puget Sound, Mackenzie wrote his name and added proudly: "From Canada, by land, the 22nd July, 1793".

Alexander Mackenzie opened up a vast territory for trading. The book he wrote about his journey was read by Thomas Jefferson, the President of the United States. He organized the Lewis and Clarke army expedition (see page 26) that crossed the continent of America to the Pacific from the middle-west more than ten years after Mackenzie crossed Canada almost on his own.

MUNGO PARK
and the course of the Niger

Mungo Park, one of thirteen children of a Scottish farmer, became a doctor and went to the Far East as a ship's surgeon. When he was only twenty-four, he was asked by the African Association to explore the course of the Niger River in north-west Africa. The African Association was formed to encourage trade with Africa.

Park set out from the mouth of the Gambia in June 1795. He was riding a horse and wearing a top hat and a blue coat—strange clothing for African exploration. But he was strong. The climate was hot, damp, and unhealthy. He had

only two day's supply of food. The negroes who started out with him slipped off or died. He struggled on alone. He received food in exchange for hairs from his beard which the natives wanted as a charm. He was robbed, beaten, and stripped of his clothing when trying to reach Timbuktu. But Park became the first white man to see and explore the Niger. When he got back to Britain, he wrote an exciting book, *Travels in the Interior of Africa.* His own drawing, below, comes from that book.

Ten years later Mungo Park led another expedition to the Niger. This time the British government supported him. He started out with forty-five Europeans, including soldiers and naval boat-builders. By the time the expedition reached the Niger three months later, most of the Europeans had died of fever. By the time a boat had been built at Sego, a trading post, only Park and four soldiers (one of them mad) survived. In sailing down the river towards Timbuktu they were attacked by natives. The mad soldier and another soldier died. At Busa Rapids natives attacked again. The boat hit a rock, and Park and the two soldiers were drowned.

MERIWETHER LEWIS and WILLIAM CLARKE

explorers of the American West

In 1804, President Jefferson asked army Captains M Lewis and W Clarke to prepare an expedition to travel up the Missouri River to its source. They were to cross the Rocky Mountains, find and follow a navigable river flowing to the Pacific Ocean.

They set out with a party of forty-five men, and spent the winter in a fort erected in the country of the Mandan Indians. Twelve men dropped out and the remaining thirty-three continued by canoes up the Missouri, with two Indian interpreters. The countryside was magnificent to see. Once Captain Lewis had to jump into a river to escape from a brown bear. Captain Lewis nearly perished in a storm: torrential rain dislodged rocks and hailstones as big as pebbles cut the men's skin.

After finding the springs of the Missouri, they began to look for the Columbia River which flowed west to the Pacific. They smoked a pipe of peace with an Indian chief, who sent ten warriors to guide the white men to the Columbia River. Their route was over difficult Indian trails. Food ran out and the horses were killed one by one for meat. On 13th September they reached a wide part of the Columbia, built canoes, and floated downriver, shooting the five-kilometre rapids of the Great Narrows on 24th October. Finally they came to the Pacific Ocean. They wintered at Merryweather Bay, and began the return journey in the spring of 1805. They reached St Louis, then on the American frontier, on 22nd May, 1806.

Lewis and Clarke and their men had covered 6,500 kilometres. They are key figures in the exploration that opened up the American West. In the 1840s families in wagon trains began to cross America from East to West to settle in California and Oregon.

Pictured above, W Clarke, and M Lewis below.

CHARLES STURT
and the Australian interior

In the first half of the nineteenth century, most of inland
Australia had still to be explored.

Captain Charles Sturt led expeditions in 1828 and 1829 to
see if the rivers of the south-east flowed into a great inland
sea as some people thought. He showed they did not.

In 1828 he discovered the Darling River, and in 1829 he
commanded an expedition that went down the Murrumbidgee
River on a whaleboat. They entered the broad Murray River
and its current took them to its mouth on 9th February, 1830.
It was a wide but shallow lake separated by sandhills from the
sea at Encounter Bay.

The return journey against the strong current was
exhausting. Food stocks were low. The men rowed from dawn
until dusk, with an hour's rest at noon: some fell asleep at the
oars. To add to their difficulties, the Murrumbidgee was in
flood. They nearly starved, but reached Sydney on 26th May,
1830, after a journey of about 3,000 km.

In 1844, Sturt led a small expedition that tried to reach the centre of Australia, but was defeated by what he named the Great Stony Desert. There was little protection from the fierce sun. Finding a small creek, they pitched tents and had to stay there for six months—"locked up . . . as effectively as if we had wintered at the Pole," Sturt wrote. Their hair ceased to grow, the lead fell out of their pencils, and the ink dried immediately on their pens. Sturt's second-in-command died of scurvy. They escaped when the first rains fell in July. Sturt made two further attempts to find fertile country but each time ran up against the desert. On the return journey he and his companions almost starved to death. A thermometer graduated to 127°F, placed in the shade, burst its bulb. When Sturt finally reached his home in Adelaide, he was so changed in appearance that his wife fainted at first sight of him.

Above, Sturt takes aim at hostile Aborigines during his epic expedition in 1830.

DAVID LIVINGSTONE
explorer and missionary in Africa

Dr David Livingstone, a Scottish medical missionary, went to Africa and became the best-known name in African exploration. On his expeditions he preferred the company of Africans; with white men he quarrelled.

In 1852–55 he explored the Zambesi River westward to the coast at Luanda, and made the return journey through Angola. Often the forests were so dense that no sunlight could penetrate. His next expedition was from the Zambesi to the east coast, during which he discovered the magnificent Victoria Falls, which the Africans called "the place of sounding smoke". He reached the coast at Quelimane, and took a ship to England. Everyone wanted to congratulate him, including Queen Victoria.

Livingstone was soon back in central Africa. He discovered Lake Nyasa and walked around its shores. He began his last expedition in 1866. He hoped to find the source of the Nile. He started out with camels, mules, buffaloes, and donkeys—but they did not survive. His men deserted or had to be sent back, until he was left with four native boys. His medicine chest was stolen. He was suffering from fever, dysentry, and appalling feet ulcers. Sick and depressed, he spent several months at Ujiji, on the eastern shore of Lake Bemba. On 10th November, 1871, a white man appeared, and said: "Dr Livingstone, I presume?" It was H M Stanley, sent to look for Livingstone by a New York newspaper.

Africa was in Livingstone's blood. He would not leave. When he started his final journey on 2nd August, 1872, he became so weak he often had to be carried on a litter. On 2nd May, 1873 at a native village, he died, kneeling by his bed. Two faithful servants wrapped him in canvas and bark, and carried him 1,500 km to Zanzibar. He is buried in Westminster Abbey.

HENRY MORTON STANLEY
and central Africa

H M Stanley was a newspaper correspondent who became a famous explorer almost by accident.

He was born John Rowlands, in Denbigh, Wales, and was orphaned at six. Brought up in a workhouse, he ran away to sea at fifteen. He worked his way to America on a ship. In New Orleans, he was befriended and adopted by a salesman called Henry Morton Stanley. Young John took his new father's name and made it world-famous.

In 1871, the *New York Herald* sent Stanley to look for Dr David Livingstone, missing in central Africa. Stanley and his Africans hacked their way through dense forests for 1,000 kilometres and found Livingstone. It was a famous meeting, with some famous words. Stanley took off his cap, and said: "Dr Livingstone, I presume?"

When Livingstone died in 1873, Stanley decided to complete the opening-up of central Africa. In 1874, newspapers financed an expedition from the east coast. Stanley showed he could survive heat, hardship, and disease. Three young Englishmen who went with him did not survive: two died of illness and one was drowned. The porters carried a boat built in five sections, on which Stanley explored the vast Lake Victoria, and also Lake Tanganyika. The porters carried the boat overland for over 300 kilometres. Stanley discovered and traced the Congo River. As the expedition went downriver, they were attacked by cannibals shouting "Meat! Meat!" Some of Stanley's men were killed and wounded; others were drowned at rapids and waterfalls. Food was short. Finally the survivors struggled through to the west coast at Boma in August, 1877. They had crossed Africa from coast to coast in 999 days.

Two years later Stanley set up trading stations along the Congo on behalf of the King of the Belgians, leading to the setting-up of the Belgian Congo Free State.

Stanley settled in England, became a member of parliament, and was knighted. He is buried in the village churchyard at Pirbright, Surrey—not beside Livingstone in Westminster Abbey as he had hoped.

ROBERT PEARY
first at the North Pole

The first leader of an expedition known to reach the North Pole was Robert Edwin Peary, an American naval officer. It was the reward for years of determined effort.

Like Roald Amundsen, conqueror of the South Pole, Peary had been fascinated with polar exploration from boyhood. He spent several years living with the Eskimos, learning how to handle their dogs and to survive in the intense cold. He organized and led eight Arctic expeditions. On his first in 1898, blizzards and frozen toes forced him back. His toes had to be cut off to save his life. On the seventh attempt in 1905–6, he got within 322 kilometres of the pole. His eighth attempt was successful.

On 22nd February, 1909 the assault party set out from Cape Columbia, in Grant Land. He had 22 men, 19 sledges, and 133 dogs. The Pole was 800 km away across the treacherous icefloes. The ice kept splitting in front of them and some of the dogs fell to their deaths. Once the whole party was marooned on an island of ice, but they escaped by constructing a bridge made of sledges.

Peary used a series of relay parties. On the final thrust he was accompanied by his negro servant, Matthew Henson, and four Eskimos; they had five sledges and forty dogs. "The sky was a colourless pall gradually deepening almost to black at the horizon, and the ice was a ghastly and chalky white," Peary wrote. They actually overshot the Pole a short way and had to return to it. It was 6th April, 1909. The final 210 km had been covered in two days—an astonishing speed without skis. His daily average over the whole distance on the polar ice has never been equalled.

Peary's success was a disappointment for Roald Amundsen, the Norwegian explorer, who switched his target from the North Pole to the South Pole. (See page 39.)

ROBERT SCOTT
and the South Pole

The British explorer, Captain Robert Falcon Scott, commanded an expedition to the South Pole which set up base at Cape Evans in January 1911. At the same time the Norwegian Roald Amundsen was also setting up a base for an assault on the Pole.

Scott started out for the Pole—1,500 km away—on Ist November, 1911. Food depots were set up along the route. 650 km from the Pole, the last of the ponies was killed for meat and the dogs were sent back to the base. The last of the

This is the Southern Cross Hut at Cape Adare, the base for Scott's 1901–4 Polar expedition.

Left to right: Bowers, Scott, Wilson, Evans, Oates.

supporting parties went back on 4th January, 1912. Scott was about 320 km from the Pole. For the final thrust, he took with him Dr E A Wilson, Captain L E G Oates, of the Inniskilling Dragoons, Lieutenant H R Bowers, and Petty-Officer Edgar Evans. On 18th January they reached the Pole—and found Amundsen's tent and the Norwegian flag flying! He had reached the Pole on 14th December. It was a crushing blow.

Blizzards and frostbite made the return a hell. Evans fell and injured himself and died on 17th February. Then on 16th March Captain Oates staggered from the tent into the blizzard, sacrificing his life rather than slow down his companions.

"We all hope to meet the end with a similar spirit, and assuredly the end is not far," Scott wrote in his diary.

The last tent was pitched on 19th March. They had neither fuel nor food. The nearest depot was only 18 km away. Scott's last diary entry was on 29th March: "It seems a pity, but I do not think I can write any more." But he had written a few days earlier: "How much better all this has been than lounging in great comfort at home." The bodies of the three explorers, in their tent, were found by a search party eight months later.

ROALD AMUNDSEN
two victories of exploration

From boyhood, the Norwegian Roald Amundsen was determined to become a polar explorer. He prepared his body by playing football and by exercising to strengthen his muscles. He prepared his mind by reading all he could find about polar exploration. "Victory awaits him who has everything in order," he said later. "Defeat is certain for him who has neglected to take the necessary precautions."

Amundsen achieved two great victories. He was the first man to sail through the North-West Passage, from the Canadian Arctic to the Pacific, which explorers had been trying to do for centuries. And he became the first man to reach the South Pole.

He had prepared to conquer the North Pole; but when he heard in April 1909 that the American Commander Peary had done it, Amundsen decided to aim for the South Pole. He kept his plans a secret until after sailing from Oslo fjord in June 1910. In January 1911, his ship the *Fram* reached the Ross Ice Barrier. In the same month the British explorer Captain R F Scott (see page 36) reached the Ross Sea with *his* expedition, knowing that a race was on. It was now that Amundsen's careful preparations were to show their worth.

Amundsen used dogs, which proved superior to Scott's ponies and dogs. His final thrust for the Pole was with four men and four sledges. The dogs were driven hard to the polar plateau, then the twenty-four weakest were shot and one of the sledges abandoned. It left six dogs to each of three sledges. With snow falling constantly, they were guided by compass. Suddenly the snow stopped and the sun shone brightly. On 14th December, 1911 Amundsen planted the Norwegian flag on the South Pole. Captain Scott found it about a month later. There was also a letter which Amundsen had written to King Haakon VII of Norway, telling him of the Norwegian victory. Scott was asked to deliver the letter, should Amundsen never reach home. Ironically, it was Scott who failed to reach home, not Amundsen.

Like Scott, Amundsen died tragically. In 1928, the Italian explorer General Nobile tried to cross the North Pole in an airship, but crashed. Amundsen set off in a seaplane to search for Nobile, but himself crashed and was never heard of again.

JACQUES-YVES COUSTEAU
undersea explorer

The other explorers in this book journeyed on the seas and overland. Captain Jacques-Yves Cousteau (pronounced ku'sto) is famous for his explorations under the sea. We can share the fascinating undersea world he has found through his photographs and his films, which have been shown on television throughout the world.

After graduating from the Naval Academy at Brest in 1930, he joined the French Navy as a midshipman. He developed an interest in "goggle diving" in 1936, and in 1943 he and Emil Gaghan invented the aqualung, a breathing device that meant a "skin diver" could go down into the sea as far as ninety metres. The diver breathes air from cylinders strapped on his back.

In 1946 Cousteau set up the Undersea Research Group, to study diving techniques and life beneath the sea. He was director of the *Calypso* Red Sea Expedition in 1951-52 and then headed a four-year exploration undersea on behalf of the National Geographic Society. During this expedition Cousteau found a Greco-Roman galley of the third century B.C. off the coast of Tunisia, which contained archaeological treasures.

In the summer of 1956, Cousteau photographed the bottom of the Atlantic Ocean at depths of seven kilometres. Special equipment had to be designed to go so deep. He worked with Professor Auguste Piccard on the construction of the bathyscaphe, a vehicle in which people could study the sea bed at great depths.

In the 1960s Cousteau led experiments called Conshelf in which men stayed for days in underwater stations. In 1963, he and seven divers lived for a month at the bottom of the Red Sea and in 1965 Cousteau directed a team of six French scientists who went down 100 metres into the Mediterranean in a spherical chamber weighing sixty tons. They stayed there twenty-two days and could leave their underwater home to explore the sea bed. Some day, Cousteau predicts, men will live in underwater cities.

In the picture, Cousteau climbs down into the diving chamber for a journey of underwater exploration.

SIR EDMUND HILLARY
and the conquest of Everest

Edmund Percival Hillary and Tensing Norgay became the best-known mountaineers in history when they climbed to the summit of Mount Everest, the world's highest mountain, in May 1953.

Hillary was born at Auckland, New Zealand, and first learned to climb in the New Zealand Alps. In 1951, he gained experience of climbing in the central Himalayas. Mount Everest stands in the eastern Great Himalayas, in a remote region on the border between Nepal and Tibet. Its icy slopes tower to 8,848 metres. Before 1953, seven attempts to conquer it had failed.

The leader of the 1953 British expedition was Colonel (now Lord) John Hunt. In the party were some Sherpas—hillmen of Eastern Nepal. One of them was Tensing Norgay. He had been on the British expeditions in the 1930s as a porter, and had made his name in the Swiss expedition of 1952.

Hunt's attack was by climbing the face of the adjoining Lhotse peak and crossing to Everest on the depression between—the South Col. Good teamwork and organization were essential. A series of camps were necessary. On 17th May, George Lowe and Wilfred Noyce set up Camp 7 on the Lhotse face, at 7,315 metres. On the 27th, Tom Bourdillon and Charles Evans reached the South Peak of Everest (8,745 metres) at one o'clock—too late in the day to risk going on. On 28th May, a camp was set up at 8,500 metres by George Lowe, Alfred Gregory and Ang Nyima. Hillary and Tensing passed the night there. At daylight, each hoisted the 13 kg of oxygen gear on to his back and began climbing. They reached the South Peak at 9 a.m. Bourdillon and Evans had described to them the last ridge. They crossed it and stood "on top of the world" at 11.30 a.m., 29th May, 1953. They embraced breathlessly and Tensing held up his ice-axe in triumph. Hillary later wrote: "My initial feelings were of relief. Relief that there were no more steps to cut, no more ridges to traverse and no more humps to tantalize us with hopes of success." Tensing made an offering of food to the gods, and Hillary laid a small crucifix into the snow. They spent about fifteen minutes admiring the unique view, then turned to leave.

Pictured above are Hillary and Tensing, photographed in Katmandu after their victory.

On 2nd June, the team were together again at the base camp at Thyangboche. That same day Queen Elizabeth II was crowned in London. The British people had two great events to celebrate. As the news was broadcast to the coronation crowds in London, loud cheers broke out. No other achievement could have been more fitting for the occasion. Everest had been conquered 101 years after its discovery, and at the eleventh attempt.

GLOSSARY

Airship A steerable balloon.

Aztecs An Indian tribe that dominated Mexico until the Spanish conquest of Cortes (1519).

Blizzard A blinding snowstorm with icy gales.

Causeway A raised roadway across wet ground or water.

Col A high pass or depression in a range of mountains.

Colonists People settled in a distant land owned by the mother country.

Conquistadors The Spanish conquerors of South America.

Course Route, direction.

Dysentery A disease with discharge of bloody mucus from the bowels, accompanied by gripping pain.

Expedition An undertaking by a number of persons involving travel, and usually hardship; the group of persons in the undertaking.

Frostbite An inflammation, usually of the fingers and toes, due to exposure to severe cold.

Incas The royal family in Peru before the Spanish conquest of Pizarro (1532).

Maroon To leave on a desolate island.

Missionary A person sent to a distant land to teach religion.

Monsoon A wind that blows in the Indian Ocean and in

southern Asia, blowing from the south-west in summer and from the north-east in winter.

Musket Muzzle-loading hand-gun that was used by foot-soldiers.

Navigable That may be voyaged on.

Navigation The act, art, or science of finding a ship's position and guiding it. Also applies to aircraft.

Navigator A person skilled in navigation; a sea explorer.

New France The French settlements along the St Lawrence River in Canada, centred on Quebec (founded 1608).

North-West Passage A way through the Canadian north from the Atlantic to the Pacific. It was sought from the sixteenth century. The complete voyage was first achieved by Amundsen in 1903-5.

Portaging Carrying goods or a boat overland, especially between one waterway and another.

Scurvy A disease caused by not eating enough fresh fruit and vegetables containing Vitamin C.

Strait A narrow passage of water connecting two seas.

Survey To measure a coast, country, and so on.

Transit The passing of a planet across the sun's disk.

Torrential Like a violent, rushing stream.

READING LIST

The Discoverers by Richard Armstrong, published by Ernest Benn, is about the voyages to find a sea route from Europe to the Indies

Explorers and Exploring by Bernard Brett, published by Kestrel books.

The Travels of Marco Polo by Bernard Brett, published by Collins.

The Ocean World of Jacques Cousteau and

Window In the Sea, both by Jacques Cousteau, are published by Angus and Robertson.

Voyages of Captain Cook by Roger Hart, published by Wayland.

Polar Deserts by Wally Herbert, published by Topic Books.

Empire to Commonwealth by R Howard, published by Wayland.

Our Everest Adventure by Lord Hunt, published by Brockhampton Press.

Livingstone in Africa by J Judd, published by Wayland.

Discovery of Australia by Rex and Thea Rienits, published by Hamlyn.

Captain Scott by David Sweetman, published by Wayland.

The Explorers by Desmond Wilcox published by the BBC.

James Cook, Scientist and Explorer by Trevor Williams, published by Priory Press, and obtainable from Wayland.

Great Polar Adventures by Marie Herbert, published by Piccolo.

Index

Picture Acknowledgements

Camera Press, 43;   Keystone Press, 41;   Mary Evans Picture Library, 9, 11, 17, 19, 28, 35;   Royal Geographical Society, 37. Other pictures belong to the Wayland Picture Library.